Schizophrenia
And
Consciousness

Schizophrenia
And
Consciousness

A Testable Hypothesis

Simeon Locke

To order additional copies of this book, contact:
Xlibris Corporation
1-888-795-4274
www.Xlibris.com
Orders@Xlibris.com
103475

CONTENTS

Chapter 1

Preface

Much of human behavior, in science as in life, is based on faith, which Paul tells us (Hebrews XI:i) is the "evidence of things not seen". More recently, this same notion has been reformulated in the familiar maxim, "Seeing is believing and vice versa". Most often we are not aware of the pernicious role such attitudes play in our thinking, so deeply are they ingrained. Cartesian dualism—the independence of body and mind—is an outstanding example. We find it embedded—often without realizing it—in such terms as "Mental Health" and "Mental Illness". Put aside the philosophical or sociological question of what constitutes illness. The separation of *mental* health and *mental* illness from physical health and illness (even our insurance coverage may do that) preserves that implicit prejudice despite almost half a century of physical based psychopharmacology.

But we persist. According to the publication *Science*, DSM-V, will discard the old subtypes of schizophrenia. Instead, diagnosis will be made on the basis of "common symptoms such as hallucinations and thought disorder" (1). Thought disorder, however, can only be inferred; as Sherrington pointed out, mind is an inference from behavior. A friend at the Princeton Institute for Advanced Studies said, "They pay me to sit and think and all they can prove is that I am sitting." Thinking is what allowed Descartes (with his dualism) to know he existed. But the observer of another does not know, cannot know, what (or that) the other thinks. Psychiatrists in their proposed DSM-V classification continue to perpetuate 17th Century dualism. If mental illness has a biological base—as almost everyone confronted with the question would admit—is it not time to acknowledge and then to relinquish our faith based preconception.

To do so, we must search for the physiologic correlates of psychiatric ilness, which induce the changes in "mind". This is difficult because physiologic processes, which are similar for all, are expressed through the individual filter of "the mind" drawing on individual memories, experiences and thoughts. Psychotic manifestations can be classified only in a most general way, with individual differences subsumed under the general rubric. The problem therefore becomes that of defining the biological mechanism of the general process that appears in the psychological expression of the individual. And the variability of the individual expression precludes obtaining statistically significant information as can be done in studying the treatment of bacterial infection or myocardial infarction.

One empirical method of attempting to define objective criteria of "psychological" disease is by the response to pharmacotherapy. Unlike psychological therapeutic techniques, psychopharmacology allows prediction of physiological mechanisms that underlie the curative aspects. But by itself the response to drug therapy is insufficient as an explanatory device; many drugs have a long history of effective use with no understanding of the mechanism of action. When coupled with anatomical observations, pharmacotherapy may serve as a presumptive starting point. The dopamine hypothesis of schizophrenia arose not only from the effect of dopamine blocking agents on the symptoms of schizophrenia but also from the observations of changes in the D_2 dopamine receptor. The problem the inference from therapy presents is the same as any conclusion drawn from the effect of a drug or a neurotransmitter: the drug or transmitter does not change behavior directly. It works by changing the function of a neuronal network. So, while it reaffirms the biological nature of the psychological process it does not define in a meaningful way the mechanism of the process. The mechanism is physiologic; it would require a physiologic technique to display it.

That problem also serves as a drawback in the use of morphologic methods. Even so called functional imaging really demonstrates only morphology (MRI) or chemistry (PET). This is further complicated by the lack of consistency of morphologic changes in schizophrenia. Increase of size of the cerebral ventricles has been reported. Decrease of size of the amygdala and of the hippocampus is noted. Reduction of the inferior parietal lobe in schizophrenic men is said to be prominent on the left side. Left posterior temporal gyrus size reduction has been observed, as have changes in right and left prefrontal areas, left inferior prefrontal region and anterior or posterior cingulate gyri. In addition, atrophy of the cerebellar vermis appears in schizophrenia. Not only is there lack of consistency in these many morphologic observations, but the question of cause and effect cannot be addressed by imaging studies. When a patient with a recent stroke has a cerebral infarct demonstrated on MRI, the causal relation seems clear; when the MRI of a patient with schizophrenia shows cerebellar vermis atrophy, it is not at all clear whether schizophrenia was the cause, the result or neither.

A dynamic physiologic method is needed. Electroencephalography will not help; the EEG of the schizophrenia patient is not sufficiently distinctive to allow differentiation. Polysomnography is inadequate. Sleep studies in schizophrenia show long sleep onset latency and reduced total sleep time, but these findings simply characterize insomnia and are not specific for schizophrenia. Decreased latency of onset of rapid eye movement sleep has also been noted, but again, this is not specific to schizophrenia, nor is it a constant finding. Perhaps most specific is a reduction of sleep spindles. Most prominent in Stage 2 sleep, spindles may occur in slow wave sleep and even in rapid eye movement sleep. Brainstem reticular discharges suppress spindle genesis; reduction of sleep spindles may indicate an active brainstem reticular system, a conclusion that would accord with the clinical observation of a hyperattentive state.

Evoked potentials perhaps offer the best dynamic measurement of the schizophrenic attentive state. Time-locked to a stimulus, the recurrent response display is intensified while the random background is algebraically cancelled by a series of repeated identical stimuli. Clearly, this is an artificial situation but it can be used as a measure of behavioral hyperawareness that cannot be measured in other ways. Evoked (or event—related) potentials are recorded electrographically from the scalp. They are reported as N (negative) or P (positive) to indicate the polarity of the response, followed by a number to indicate the time in milliseconds of appearance. Because the brain is a volume conductor responses generated at great distances from the cortical surface—as far as brainstem—can be recorded by scalp electrodes. Responses during the first 14 ms arise below the thalamus. The first cortical component is a negative response at 20 ms (N20). It is an early event related response uninfluenced by attention. It is subliminal—that is awareness cannot be verbalized. The subject is unaware of its occurrence, if awareness is measured by verbalization. Even in the presence of so-called unawareness, the stimulus may affect behavior so awareness exists at some level. What is lacking is awareness of awareness which is objectively identified not only by verbalization but by the appearance of a late event related potential which may appear as late as 300 ms or more after delivery of the stimulus.

On the basis of behavior, one might predict the lack of a late event related potential results from an inhibitory process—a behavioral, not a cellular inhibition. The prediction would be that inhibition is most likely of cortical origin—a cortical inhibition of a cortical response. On occasion, the undetected stimulus may be brought to awareness as a result of increasing intensity or by the comments of another; in either situation one realized the stimulus had been noted earlier and had been suppressed. In the period between the early and the late event related potentials—as much as half a second—the initial response (not yet recognized) is being operated on in buffer storage to be brought to conscious awareness or to be suppressed. In this early stage considerable analysis is taking place. The early events in a sensory chain participate in analysis, identification, selection and a sorting of stimuli. The early event related potential represents a preperceptual phase, in the sense that the stimulus may produce a behavioral response independent of recognition of the percept. That is, the awareness of the percept cannot be verbalized.

If the schizophrenic patient is hyperaware, as clinical observation suggests, evoked potential measurements may offer an objective physiologic method to verify it. With objective demonstration of a hyperattentive state, many other symptomatic manifestations of the process might be better understood. Hallucinations, paranoia, tangentiality, flight of ideas, klang association might all be shown to have a unifying mechanism. They might all relate to the fact that the schizophrenic patient sees too much, hears too much and is overloaded with stimuli (which most of us discard) that intrude on life.

Chapter 2

Schizophrenia

Schizophrenia, a "splitting of the psychic functions" was described by Bleuler in his 1911 text as an inability to distinguish reality from fantasy. He construed this to be an impairment of perception of reality. Although the names of the subtypes have changed, his basic classification persists. Two-thirds of the cases appear between the ages of 17 and 25, somewhat earlier in boys than in girls. The cause is not known. The turbulence of adolescence with associated hormonal and emotional changes has been blamed. Genetic causes have been implicated as have a variety of other factors—intrauterine, developmental, environmental, physical or psychological. But we really do not know.

Symptoms have been classified as positive and negative. Disturbance of mood and behavior is common to both groups. Positive symptoms are an intensification or exaggeration of things that appear in the normal individual; abnormalities of perception, hallucinations, problems with inferential thinking, delusions, disorganization of ideas, tangentiality in language thought to represent flight of ideas, word salad and klang association—the production of language on the basis of sound rather than meaning. Negative symptoms reflect a diminution or absence of phenomena that occur in the normal: avolition, lack of goal directed behavior, decrease of fluency thought to reflect a decrease of ideas, blunting of affect and lack of attention to and involvement with the environment. Motor manifestations in the form of catatonia with perseveration of posture, rigidity, immobility and so-called waxy flexibility may appear in the negative syndrome.

Separated from the positive and negative symptom complexes is a third group called cognitive. Intelligence is normal, orientation is intact, but reality may be misinterpreted. Circumstantiality, tangentiality, condensation of separate items, illogicality, parcellation of thoughts, distortion of conceptual relations, substitution of parts for wholes, and difficulty separating relevant from irrelevant may all be features of the cognitive form of schizophrenia. You can understand why Freud quotes Hughlings Jackson as saying, "Find out all about dreams and you will have found out all about insanity."

In the positive syndrome, the behavior of the schizophrenic patient suggests an intrusion of environmental stimuli most people neglect or discard. Its manifestation is prominent in language and suggests a far broader influence of which speech is representative. The intrusion may occur at an early processing stage but how early (and how far peripheral) cannot be determined on the basis of behavior alone. Processing of stimuli occurs at early stages in many sensory systems. In the visual system, retinal ganglion cells of the frog behave as "bug receptors" [2] exhibiting orientation specificity of movement similar to that exhibited by many (but not all) mammals [3]. Cortical columns in primary visual area V_1 are orientation specific; movement area output joins with output of other visual areas (for color, object and other aspects of vision) to effect a unified percept to which is added "awareness" (words are inadequate here for there is no current terminology by which the concept can be expressed). If distorted, it may distort the distinctive features of the percept. This kind of perceptual interaction is not restricted to a single modality as the example from vision might suggest. It may be cross modal or multimodal. Think of audio analgesia in which sound can block perception of (? reaction to) pain, or the gating produced by large fiber sensory stimulation (conducted in posterior spinal tracts) of small fiber neurons that conduct pain to ventrolateral spinal pathways.

An organism is constantly bombarded by an extraordinary number of sensory stimuli. In order to act coherently most stimuli must be discarded or suppressed so as not to generate responses. They are filtered out before reaching "consciousness". This does not mean they are not available to the organism. Rather, they are available but not attended to. Focused attention relegates them to the periphery. They become part of the ambient surround perhaps as part of behavioral context but not as a driving force of action. These peripheral stimuli are present but behaviorally inhibited. The behavioral inhibition that occurs in most subjects must be distinguished from cellular inhibition, an active neuronal process. That it is not cellular and that it occurs at a comparatively high level is indicated by the frequent ability of the normal individual to retrieve the suppressed stimulus after the fact. The metaphor employed to deal with the phenomenon is the focusing of attention. It is as if attention embraces the entire ambient environment but that a central cone occupies and is focused on the major area of concern. The periphery is available for retrieval but requires additional impetus. In schizophrenia, it is as if the focus were not sufficiently narrow. The wider cone allows stimuli from a wider field to rise to the level of self-consciousness. How behavioral inhibition is imposed and how it is removed is not known and is one of the major questions about attention. Indeed the whole subject of attention and whether it is distinguished from or is a part of (or identical with) consciousness is still open for consideration. What does seem likely however is that the behavioral suppression of cortical awareness of a stimulus is also a cortical and probably a higher level, function. That is, suppression is top down. In contrast, the response to the stimulus is bottom up and may relate less to the modality specific aspect of the stimulus than to the nonspecific input associated with it. What this means is that a stimulus need not be intensified in order to intrude on consciousness. A subliminal stimulus may exceed threshold if the nonspecific input associated with it (but induced by collaterals of another modality) is increased. The other modality need not be recognized if, as in the case of vestibular function, its specific and nonspecific aspects can be dissociated. Because the vestibular system has a balanced input (that is, the input of one vestibule is measured against the input of the other) the specific input may be low at a time the nonspecific input is high. That increases awareness of and attention to ordinarily irrelevant input from the ambient surround with intrusion into consciousness. This is a mechanism postulated to be at work in schizophrenia.

The intensification of normal perception in the schizophrenia patient is postulated to be a manifestation of abnormal gain setting by the brainstem ascending reticular activating system. This widely distributed neuronal system, now known to extend beyond brainstem into hypothalamus and basal forebrain, is influenced by light, which entrains the clock that controls the sleep-wake cycle. It projects widely to cortex to arouse or activate it and make it ready to receive stimuli from the environment. It receives signals from the environment by way of collateral input from each of the classic sensory systems. These specific systems transmit information about the various sensations that have served as stimuli. Each pathway conducts information about one modality only; the visual pathways conduct information only about vision, the gustatory pathways transmit information only about taste. The collaterals from each of the primary sensory pathways however lose the modality indicators when contributed to the activating system and serve only the arousal mechanism. The distinction between sight and sound, smell and taste, which is maintained in the first set of pathways—called lemnisci because they are discrete bundles of fibers unlike those of the reticular activating system where the fibers are loosely aggregated and widely distributed—is lost on the collateral branches. Input to the activating system is the same no matter with which modality it has originated; it functions independent of the sensory system with which it started and is now in the service of arousal.

Light serves an important role as a sensory modality contributing to the arousal system. Its role would be independent (in addition to) its function in setting the circadian clock. The suprachiasmatic nucleus of the hypothalamus functions as a master clock to entrain the independent clocks of other cells which in turn determine such things as hormone cycles, glucose metabolism, lipogenesis, leptin responsiveness and obesity, feeding cycles and more. Cycles are initiated in part in non-image-forming retinal ganglion cells. But light has a more immediate arousal effect, independent of the circadian clock, presumably by direct input (by way of collaterals) to the ascending reticular activating system. Presumably these collaterals derive from image-forming or image-conducting pathways with immediate contribution and therefore immediate on-off function. The contribution of light to the ascending reticular activating system may not account for the proposed high setting of the gain of arousal, but it would help understand the effect of light on schizophrenia behavior—particularly language. Some years ago, we measured the amount of talk by schizophrenia patients in the light and in the dark. There was a striking increase in the ratio of talk in a lighted environment when compared with the amount of talk in the dark. Schizophrenic patients were more influenced by the light than were aphasics or dements. How much of this is a manifestation of the nonspecific light input and how much reflects the effects of the percepts of the visual environment cannot be judged. Behaviorally, they are inseparable; increasing the effect of one will simultaneously increase the effect of the other.

If the arousal system is overactive, as is postulated for schizophrenia, the patient becomes hyperaware. Stimuli that are normally suppressed intrude on awareness. The schizophrenic patient may be aware of things in the environment of which the normal observer is unaware. Because of the asymmetric relationship between patient and observer, the "normal" stimuli that reach consciousness in the patient are termed hallucinations—one of the cardinal positive symptoms of schizophrenia—by the observer.

A hallucination is defined as a percept in the absence of an appropriate external sensory stimulus. It is distinguished from illusion in which an environmental stimulus is misinterpreted and perceived as different from reality. With the advent of psychotropic medication, hallucinations have become less common and more difficult to study. Two interesting questions arise with respect to them. First, where are they generated, and are they internally derived or do they represent misinterpretation of external events? Second, wherever generated, does the report of the hallucination correspond directly to the sensory (perceptual) experience, or is it an interpretation of the sensation or percept? That is, does the nervous system operate on the sensory input to construct percepts that are only tangentially related to the input? We have all had visions of things that were not there—momentary illusions. But these differ from schizophrenic hallucinations in that they immediately self correct. I see a dark movement low down in the periphery of my visual field (or even an immobile object) and identify it as my dog (even though I know my dog is elsewhere), to recognize immediately as my macula captures the item, what it actually is. Like so many "hallucinations" in non-schizophrenic states, (toxic, metabolic, epileptic) the false item is visual; in schizophrenia, it is most often auditory. The occurrence in the normal of what occurs in psychosis suggests a general principle; the parallelism testifies that schizophrenia is not a disorder introduced from without. Like most neurologic illnesses (and unlike bacterial pneumonia for example where the pathogen comes from outside), symptoms are uncovered by the lesion and display something inherent in the nervous system. What makes the schizophrenic hallucination pathologic is its intensity and its duration. It need not be mistaken for reality, although it often is and like the hallucination in the normal may carry with it an affective cloak; how often are we startled—even frightened—by an unanticipated, ill-defined movement (for example) in the periphery of the visual field.

Whether generated from within or stimulated from without, the hallucination often contains information from the individual's life and has a sort of internal logic. In this respect, it resembles a dream, which can be construed as the analog of a hallucination in the nonpsychotic individual, with its flight of ideas, its tangentiality. Yet, it too has an internal logic and though generated from within contains information from the individual's outer life. The relation of external stimuli to the formation and fabric of the psychotic hallucination can only be speculative for objective validation is almost impossible to obtain. In part, this is because, during the psychotic episode, the patient is not able to indicate the external source; in part this is because the objective observer usually will not be aware of the stimulus. Evidence therefore must be anecdotal; statistical analysis is not possible. On rare occasions, the recovered patient can retroactively report the experience. A particularly good example appears in Virginia Woolf's, "Mrs. Dalloway". Woolf was specially qualified as she had suffered periods of what she called "madness"'; these were clearly recognized as hallucinatory psychotic episodes. In her novel, Septimus Warren Smith, back from the war, suffers episodic psychotic hallucinations. In one, which Woolf describes at length, Smith alternates rapidly between environmental input (roses, traffic sounds, the sound of a penny whistle) and the hallucination, which incorporates the environmental input (roses, pillars of sound that become visible). The strength of this report is that the observer and the observed are the same individual viewing both sides of the situation simultaneously.

An example from my own experience is less conclusive (for the observer can only infer) but is strongly suggestive. On our ward in a State Psychiatric Hospital, we had a young woman who had been diagnosed as schizophrenic. She had been medication free for some months. She often heard her father, who worked far away in a laundry, talking to her. It was not possible to get a clear report from her as to what he said but it was apparently without a frightening or accusatory tone. One evening I was working quite late in my office on the top (fifth) floor of the medical building where our patients had individual rooms. The ward was quiet; patients had been put to bed. As I worked, I heard sounds coming from the heating duct. They were clearly human voices although unintelligible. They were obviously coming from below, as we were the uppermost level. Patients on the four floors below presumably had been put to bed. In the basement was the laundry with its noisy night crew. Could the sounds be coming up from the *laundry*? Could my patient have conflated the hospital laundry with her father's laundry, the hospital voices with her father's voice? I had worked at that hospital for several years and never before heard those sounds. I had never before duplicated that patient's experience, so clearly the voices she heard were a hallucination.

This is not to insist that all schizophrenic hallucinations are externally originated. It is simply to point out that during a psychotic episode, the patient seems hyperattentive, extremely vulnerable to external stimuli that would be irrelevant or suppressed by the non-psychotic individual—a point to which we will return for demonstration by more objective methods.

Most often, the hallucination is accompanied by an affective association—often unpleasant. This component, whether the hallucination is a reflection of an external event or not, is clearly generated from within, just as the affective aspect of a normal percept is internal. A gray day is sad, a sunny day is cheerful. The sadness is not in the gray, not in the day, but in the individual, perhaps as a result of accumulated experiences, stored memories, previous acquisitions. This is but a reiteration of the old distinction between perception and apperception, which, like the distinction between internally and externally generated, may be artificial.

How trustworthy is the schizophrenic patient's report of the hallucination? This second question relates even if only tangentially to the issue of apperception for apperception sculpts not merely the affective aspect of an experience but also the perceptual (in the strict sense). The nervous system operates on its input to shape it and the shape represents—at least in part—the structure (and therefore the function) of the neural networks which may represent previous experience particularly if acquired during a critical period. It is almost impossible to obtain raw data when the schizophrenic reports a hallucination. Some of this responsibility rests with us. We ask (as I have written elsewhere) (4), "Are you hearing voices?" Shouldn't we ask, "Are you hearing something?" Follow up to the acknowledgement should not be, "What are the voices saying?" but "What are you hearing?" The usual reply to the confrontational question is never raw data—the actual words; it is a summary statement, a formulation: "Bad things." or "They are calling me names." For me, this raises the question as to whether the sounds are inchoate, unstructured and overlaid with an affective cloak. The interpretation is "bad things".

Perhaps some information about this can be obtained from a study of hallucinations that result from the brain stimulation that occurs in epileptic seizures. Often associated with a temporal lobe focus, these hallucinations may be auditory or visual. The reports may be of structured experiences, but careful exploration of the sort that is not possible in schizophrenic patients reveals a distinction between the raw data of the experience and the elaborated report. For example, I had one patient who had posttraumatic temporal lobe seizures that were initiated with a visual aura. He reported seeing little people in brightly colored hats jitterbugging vigorously in the far periphery of his visual field. When I explored this with him, it became clear that what he saw was poorly defined brightly colored movement. When he turned to look at it to bring the dancing people into focus, it would, of course, move as he turned and remain in the periphery. He was never able to bring his macula to the scene to visualize it clearly. The notion of people, hats and dancing was imposed on the vision as an "explanation", an interpretation, an operation of the nervous system.

A second patient, a young Greek man, had a temporal glioblastoma that produced seizures introduced with a musical aura. When asked what the music was he identified it as either Tchaikovsky or a Greek folk song, he couldn't be sure which. This inability to identify must mean that the music was not clearly defined (or remembered) and the uncertain identification was a reconstruction perhaps occasioned by the affective as well as the acoustic aspects.

I understand the schizophrenic hallucination to be a physiologic event, often released by an external stimulus of which the patient is aware, but which does not come to awareness in the observer. It is given an explanation or rationale as well as an affective coloring by the patient's nervous system based on previously accumulated memories, percepts and emotions. The action of the external trigger, which is the pivotal aspect, represents a heightened awareness in the schizophrenic patient that is evident in behaviors other than hallucinations and may constitute a fundamental physiological abnormality in the disorder. Curiously, this is rarely noted in reports of schizophrenic symptoms although overinclusiveness is commented on [5]. This heightened awareness has been noted in relation to evoked potential studies. "Successful processing of sensory input requires the ability to inhibit intrinsic responses to redundant stimuli and reciprocally to facilitate responses to less frequent salient stimuli. There is evidence to suggest that both these processes are 'impaired' in schizophrenia" [6].

What remains unexplained is why the schizophrenic hallucination is generally auditory in contrast to other hallucinatory states: in normals (hypnogogic, hypnopompic and even dreams), epileptic and toximetabolic.

Delusions constitute a second major positive symptom of schizophrenia. A delusion is defined as a fixed, dominating mental conception resistant to reason with regard to reality. This sounds rather like Paul's definition of faith, but faith, he states, is "the substance of things hoped for", and delusional material is not usually hoped for; rather it is frightening, troublesome and to be avoided. Like hallucinations, delusions are composed of two components—one sensory (or perceptual), a second affective. The sensory component may come from the environment, (either internal or external) and the affective component comes from within the nervous system. In hallucinations normal sensory functions, understandable to the observer, predominate. Voices are something we have all heard. In delusions, the symptom is often outside of normal experience; control by radiowaves, for example, is unfamiliar to most of us. Should this imply there is no sensory input to the delusional ideation? Perhaps affective sensations are generated initially, then look for something (an explanation) on which to impose themselves. Like "free floating anxiety" which may come to rest on some trivial object. We know that disembodied sensations may occur in seizures or with brain stimulation (7).

Often there is an internal logic in the delusional system not evident in the product without careful dissection. So, for example, a schizophrenic man who had persistent athetosis as a manifestation of his tardive dyskinesia, when asked why he kept moving his hands, explained that it was a sign of royalty. When pressed, he stated that everyone in the Royal Family did it. When asked why, he explained, "It's in our blood." When I insisted he tell me more he became annoyed and said, "You know! It's from the medicine." Run the "delusions" backward. He knew the dyskinesia was from the medication. He knew the medication was in his blood. That made his blood different. What kind of blood is different? Royal blood of course, so everyone in the Royal Family had this dyskinetic sign of different blood. Conclusion: His movement disorder was a sign of royalty.

Paranoid ideation, often part of a delusional system, may be of a different origin. Observations suggest that schizophrenic patients see too much, hear too much. Their attention systems are less focused than in others and the ambient surround intrudes. Stimuli that are suppressed or ignored by most come to awareness in the schizophrenic. What this may do is interfere with the unity or coherence of a percept because of information overload. Fragments of a percept remain fragments. One method of controlling information overload is by grouping components, by putting a larger meaning on them. If the components of a face, for example, are subsumed under the rubric of "angry" rather than separate eyes, nose and mouth, the information input becomes less overwhelming. This will not explain all of paranoia, which appears to be intrinsic to the human nervous system and is released by various non-schizophrenic conditions such as dementia. Even a peripheral abnormality, without associated deterioration of central mechanisms may evoke a paranoid delusion. A not unfamiliar example is the hard of hearing person who is certain that others whose conversation is inaudible are talking about him.

Withdrawal, too, may be a method of dealing with information overload. When the input becomes overwhelming, one effective response to it is to cease to participate. By blocking the response to input the stimulus becomes ineffective, loses it's meaning (Sherrington's term was "adequacy") and is no longer a stimulus. So, information overload can be controlled by withdrawal. Nonparticipation is reflected in the flattening of affect that is described, with affect meaning an external expression of internal mood.

Flight of ideas, tangentiality, and klang association are often considered schizophrenic manifestations of ideation; but they are really only language which may reflect ideas, may produce ideas, or may be unrelated to ideas. If the schizophrenic patient is hyperattentive in an unfocused way a reflection of this may appear in language and result (or not) in "flight of ideas". Klang association is a cardinal example. The sound (klang) of the word stimulates the production of a similar sounding word without reference to meaning or to coherence. "When you see brown you turn around and say what town", says my schizophrenic patient. The sound of a word serving as a stimulus for another word also occurs in the normal in which duplicative use of an unusual word may catch the listener's ear without interrupting coherence as it might in the schizophrenic. I heard a distinguished professor of neurology use the unexpected non-philosophical word "phenomenological" in a lecture to be followed two or three sentences later by "phenomenological" in a different context. I knew where the second "phenomenological" had come from, although I did not know the origin of the first. This normal, and schizophrenic, reiterative phenomenon may account for echolalia and palilalia which occur in schizophrenia as they do in other neurological diseases (Parkinsonism is an outstanding example) and even in normals. Perhaps this is simply disinhibition of "echo neurons", the auditory counterpart of mirror neurons, an example of a sound stimulating a sound as in klang. But where does the first articulation come from? Man is a visual animal. Speech production in the schizophrenic is much greater in the light than in the dark as our early studies with Caplan and Kellar demonstrated [8]. Visual input stimulates an initial spoken word, which in turn stimulates further spoken words. And that visual input (it is not limited to vision; ambient sound may serve although less often than vision) reflects the hyperattentive state that precludes separation into relevant and irrelevant stimuli. We sit at a coffee table in my office on which, among other things, is the Journal of Comparative Neurology, published at the time by the Wistar Institute. It is not prominent, not an item of interest; just one of many things on the table. My schizophrenic guest talks about getting a *comparatively* small lunch in *Worcester.* An overheard airplane, which I did not realize I had heard until she called it to my attention by singing a fragment of "Coming in on a Wing and Prayer" a World War II song. These physiologic sensory stimuli evoke behavior responses that are interpreted by the normal observer to be "flight of ideas" (dualism) and tangentiality, perhaps because the observer did not "observe" the stimulus.

Insofar as a single factor can be identified as unifying the symptoms of schizophrenia, intrusion of stimuli from the ambient environment should be considered. Stimuli which normally do not reach the level of self-consciousness may initiate hallucinations or serve as the trigger for flight of ideas, tangentiality and klang association. Once released a response may then serve as the stimulus for further response (as in Brun's ataxia) best seen (heard) in klang association. Metaphorically, the focus of attention is not sufficiently narrow or the filter not specifically set. The "pathology interferes with the filtering-out of the irrelevant primes and/or the management of the interference they induce" [9]. This hyperawareness is simply an amplification of a normal process as when the unnoticed environmental "noise" is called to the "attention" of the normal individual (the airplane in my conversation with the schizophrenic patient). Whether the hyperawareness is an increase of function of the arousal system or a lack of behavioral inhibition (or both) cannot be determined by observation alone.

The importance of language in the behavior of the schizophrenic patient helps make the transition to a discussion of consciousness, for language may be required and responsible for self-consciousness. It is the only behavioral means by which self-consciousness can be evaluated. The subject must be able to say, "I know", or more accurately, "I know I know". This does not exclude mechanisms other than language as providing a base for self-consciousness; but language is the only behavioral objective measure (which also may be used to deceive).

Chapter 3

Consciousness

Whether an increase of arousal or a decrease of inhibition, hyperawareness points up the difficulties created by a consideration of consciousness. These difficulties arise, as I see it, from the lack of a disciplined definition. The lack of a disciplined definition is a consequence of the dynamic and shifting aspects of the entity which is not a tangible circumscribed object. Consciousness is a function—a process performed by neuronal networks. Its manifestations are markers of its existence; they do not define it, but they are customarily employed as descriptive. The result is a tautology. Defining a process by its manifestations contributes little to understanding. Particularly when the manifestations are as poorly circumscribed as the concept being defined. To define consciousness in terms of awareness is not only circular but demands a definition separate from consciousness of awareness. Most of us handle the problem by ignoring it. We cannot define consciousness but we are certain we know what it is.

As a working definition, consciousness may be defined as the ability of a biological system to respond to environmental stimuli. The environment is conceived as three concentric tubes (the viscera, the body wall and the surrounding world) connected respectively to the central nervous system by three sets of transducers (interoceptors, proprioceptors, and exterceptors), which deliver information to the derivatives of the three embryonic layers (germinal, mantle and marginal) the centrally placed autonomic system (hypothalamus, intermediolateral horn cells) intermediately placed nuclear masses (striatum, pallidum), and external bark, (the cortical ribbon). The response to stimuli from the three environments need not be immediate (as is the spinal reflex). It may be facultative—delayed or deferred. This definition is incomplete, for a spinal reflex would not be considered a conscious response. So, the notion of cerebral (perhaps even cortical) participation should be included.

Consciousness is a biological state. It is present in humans, probably present in other animals, and may be present in plants. Plants and even unicellular organisms give manifestations of communication. Communication means a message, information, which in turn means awareness of something by the signaling organism. If consciousness means awareness and if communication signals awareness, consciousness becomes a manifestation of life itself. Communication without intent to communicate is not incompatible with consciousness. It simply indicates lack of self consciousness in organisms lower in the evolutionary scale. All would agree that human consciousness is certainly different from that of a fish, a plant, a bacterium. There are degrees or levels of consciousness.

Human consciousness should be divided into transitive and intransitive forms. As in grammar, the transitive form requires an object, the intransitive form is limited to the subject. Consciousness can exist in an undirected way, as a state of readiness to respond in the absence of anything to respond to. A definition of intransitive consciousness would be the state of consciousness not of consciousness itself; the closest term might be vigilance, but that would extend vigilance from its usual meaning to the sleeping state, for when asleep one is still conscious. Unlike awareness, vigilance does not require an object.

Transitive consciousness should, in turn, be divided in two. In the earlier form (it comes first in time) the stimulus or percept may produce a behavioral effect without the subject being able to verbalize its presence. A stimulus of that character is customarily referred to as subliminal but that is clearly a misnomer. The fact that it produces a behavioral effect indicates that it has crossed a limen and that the organism is aware of it. This awareness is what qualifies it as a stimulus; a stimulus is a physical event that produces a response. Without a response it remains only a physical event. This kind of awareness occurs at many levels of the human nervous system. A spinal reflex (for example) is a response to a stimulus at the lowest central nervous system level. The response indicates the organism is aware (at some level) yet one would hardly argue that response constitutes consciousness, if only because the spinal reflex may persist in patients who are clinically unconscious. Criteria other than just response need to be added to properly delimit consciousness. The spinal reflex response, like all low-level responses, is obligate. Each time the stimulus is presented, a stereotyped response must occur (although aspects of the response may vary on occasion as an expression of changes in physiologic background conditions) Three additional criteria could be added to help define consciousness: 1) The processing of the stimulus is at a cortical level. This can be demonstrated objectively by event related potentials recorded from the scalp in artificial controlled circumstances. 2) Obligate response does not occur. The response may appear promptly, may be delayed or deferred or may not occur. The respondent has choice, from which arises the whole philosophical discussion of free will. 3) Stereotypy of the response disappears. On separate stimulus occasions different responses may occur. Independence from the stimulus is beginning to be demonstrated in the variability of the response, the extreme expression of which will be the internally generated external response—the self generated stimulus. This level of cortical performance underscores the paradox (perhaps only a demonstration of the paucity of linguistic expression) created by the word awareness, for at this cortical level the subject is aware, as indicated by nonverbal behavior and unaware as indicated linguistically. It can be termed consciousness with that term limited to this level of performance.

This is a comparatively low level of performance, even though it is cortical. The mature human nervous system recapitulates—anatomically and physiologically—the evolutionary development of nervous systems. The first part to develop in the human individual is the first part to develop in evolution. Subsequent acquisitions are serially applied until the last acquisition—the exuberant cerebral cortex of man which continues to develop into early adulthood—is achieved. What this means is that a peripheral stimulus, as it ascends from the lowest to the highest neural level, recapitulates in its travel (and therefore in time) an analog of neurological evolution. Consciousness without ability to verbalize awareness is a cortical function that antedated the development of self-consciousness, a term indicating consciousness of itself or consciousness of consciousness, and is probably shared by nonhuman animals lower on the phylogenetic scale, although just how far down this goes would be only a guess.

Self-consciousness—consciousness of consciousness—is the highest elaboration (although the possibility of infinite recursion—consciousness of consciousness of consciousness—is evident) and a correlate of the most elaborated cortical development. It is a late acquisition ontogenetically as well as phylogenetically and must require some symbol system to allow its representation and realization. The percept, which is required for consciousness, (in order to be consciousness of something) is no longer necessary for self-consciousness. The percept can be replaced by a concept; the object is now internally generated. This implies the presence of some sort of symbol system. It may be language; language and self-consciousness seem to develop in parallel. But other symbolic systems might work equally well precluding the conclusion that self-consciousness is exclusively human. Other animals with other symbol systems may have access to self-consciousness. Percepts which we presumably share with other animals consist of neurological models of objective reality; awareness that generates behavior is a recognition of these models. Conceptualization—revisualization in the broadest sense of the term—is a representation of the model; it is a model of a model, an awareness of awareness, or a consciousness of consciousness. The model of the model is the concept of the percept.

The concept is at the pinnacle of the input hierarchy. Sensory fragments seem to be introduced individually and then combine to form a percept which is abstracted to produce a concept. Each step in the progression takes place at a higher (that means later evolved) phylogenetic and ontogenetic level. Sensation is represented in thalamus, perception early in cortex, conception at higher cortical levels. The visual system is a good example of the process. Movement, orientation, color, object are individually represented in separate cortical areas. The output of these separate areas are ultimately combined to form a unified percept; the separate sensory components "coalesce" to become a red Ford traveling west. How this is done is not known, and is spoken of as the binding problem. Similarly, the nature of the extraction of the percept to form the concept is not known, although language is an obvious candidate. In the visual system revisualization offers a non-linguistic mechanism for conceptualization.

Just as the percept models reality (and is not biologically isomorphic with it) so the concept models the percept and language models the concept. In the final analysis, language models reality and is obviously not isomorphic with it. Among its other functions is a symbol system that represents the concept; it does not represent the percept directly. The percept must undergo transition to its abstraction—its essence or distinctive features—(the concept) before it can be transformed to the symbol system of language.

What this means is that the verbalization that is required for and is indicative of self-consciousness is a stand in for conceptualization. It indicates the stimulus to which the organism is responding has gotten beyond the perceptual stage. It has been abstracted, reformulated and perhaps given new (or additional) meaning. As a preconceptual percept it can function as a stimulus to generate behavior without an associated verbalizable concept. But for self-awareness, it must progress to the conceptual level. All of this is more than just philosophical musings; it has a physiological manifestation—the late event related potential.

Chapter 4

Evoked Potentials

In its course from periphery to cortex a group of electrical signals that represent a percept is generated by neurological transducers—receptor cells such as retinal rods and cones, auditory hair cells and somasthenic tactile corpuscles—and is conducted centrally by a series of neurological pathways with junctions at ascending levels. The junctions are waystations (nuclei) at which impulses are transferred from one nerve bundle to another. The travel of this compound electrical impulse though rapid takes time and can be recorded from the scalp at a distance from its origin. The serially appearing waveforms detected at the scalp indicate the location of the approaching electrical impulse at serial moments in time. The early waves appear at lower levels of the neuraxis (brain stem for example), late waves at higher levels, where the terms higher and lower mean physiologic (particularly in the case of cortex) as well as anatomic. Transitive consciousness is accompanied by an early event related potential; verbalization of the presence of the stimulus is usually not possible. Self-consciousness is correlated with the appearance of the late event related potential; the stimulus can be acknowledged and described.

A cortical response to a stimulus may occur without the subject being aware of it in the sense that it cannot be verbalized. Physiologic and behavioral evidence of response may exist and the participant may recognize the behavioral responses without recognizing the existence of the stimulus. The objective physiologic evidence includes the cortical evoked potential not followed by late event related potentials [10]. This consciousness without awareness is distinguished from the higher level of self-consciousness—consciousness of itself or consciousness of consciousness. This is the level at which the participant can verbalize "I know" and is accompanied by cortical late event related potentials. The P300 response (270-400 mS) has been studied extensively in schizophrenia, but not so far as I know with relation to isolated subliminal stimuli. The paradigm using subliminal stimuli has been visual or auditory but always with reference to masking which has been simultaneous, backward or forward. To test the hypothesis of hyperattentive behavior masking should not be necessary. A problem that arises is that the P300 response is generally accepted as a marker for consciousness (really for self-consciousness) but may occur in normals in response to subliminal stimuli in whom the activation is "small and brief" [11].

In order for event potentials to be recorded, they must be time-locked to the stimulus. This can be achieved by creating an artificial situation in the laboratory. Percepts representing events of daily life are not available for study. So the laboratory obtained event related potential becomes a surrogate for what goes on in the real world without absolute certainty that daily behavior follows the same internal pattern. Clinical observation therefore provides an important supplement to electrophysiology.

Behavioral observation has a distinguished tradition in clinical medicine. At the same time objective criteria, particularly if measurable give verification to the subjective clinical impression. In schizophrenia evoked potentials have been used. Customarily auditory evoked potentials are employed. What is not clear—particularly in view of the fact that hallucinations in schizophrenia are usually auditory—is whether uncovered abnormalities are unique to the auditory system or are representative of a more generalized process. If more generalized, is it an affection of multiple specific lemniscal systems or is a widespread effect of a more diffuse reticular system? Arousal and attentional systems certainly participate in evoked potentials (even if these represent lemniscal input). In the laboratory, efforts are made to control for them with such procedures as distraction. In addition, multiple modalities have been used. The evocation of some early event related potentials in sleep or coma indicates that these, perhaps in contrast to late event related potentials, do not depend on complete functioning of the activating system. In either case, is the process excitatory (perhaps of an inhibitory system as in the case of prepulse inhibition or P50 auditory suppression) or inhibition of the test response? Normal sensory processing requires either amplification of the intended stimulus, suppression of irrelevant stimuli (the ambient surround) or both. Finally, the question of where the process is generated cannot be solved unequivocally, for a downstream abnormality may be reflected by a cortical evoked potential. One study concludes that the dysfunction in schizophrenia occurs as early as the thalamus and possibly during brainstem processing of auditory responses [12]. Three major auditory techniques have been used to study evoked response in schizophrenia: 1.Mismatch negativity (MMN). 2. Prepulse inhibition (PPI). 3. P50 suppression (P50). In addition, P300, alleged to be a marker for cognitive processing has been investigated [13].

1—MMN is a measure of deviance detection and might be considered an indication of how well attention is focused. It is thought to be an automatic process (not under the patient's control). Amplitude of the response is a function of the disparity (pitch or duration) between the test stimulus and the standard. It has been obtained in comatose patients. It is therefore considered "pre-attentive" which does not preclude an influence (focus) by the attentional mechanism. MMN is generated in primary and secondary auditory cortex [14]. A standard tone, (say 1000 Hz) is repeated at a brief interval (say 0.5 sec) with injection infrequently (say 10% of the time) of a deviant tone (either in pitch or in duration). In the normal control, a major negative deflection is evoked by the stimulus at 100-200 mS following a pitch stimulus. Amplitude of the response is a function of the disparity (pitch or duration) between the test stimulus and the standard. In schizophrenia the test response is strikingly smaller with a reported mean effect size of about 1.0.

2—PPI: A sudden acoustic stimulus will normally elicit a startle response that can be inhibited by an antecedent (30-300 mS) weaker pre-stimulus. Startle may also be evoked by abrupt visual or tactile stimuli. The motor response used in the experimental paradigm is the blink evoked by the stimulus. Contraction of the orbicularis oculi is recorded electrographically. Like MMN the startle response is pre-attentive. Protocols vary but typically consist of a weak prepulse followed in 30-120 mS by a robust sound burst. In the normal the startle response is strikingly inhibited following a prepulse. In the schizophrenic patient with normal startle responses to unconditioned stimuli, the response following a prepulse is less inhibited than in the control indicating the central nervous system to be overly responsive in confirmation of behavioral observations of "distractability" [15]. PPI abnormality, present in the acute phase, has been reported to improve as symptoms of schizophrenia subside [16]. Abnormal PPI is mediated by the effect of the pedunculopontine nucleus on the nucleus reticularis pontis caudalis [17]. The role of these nuclei in the arousal—activating axis (and therefore in the attentional or distractability sphere) is to promote wakefulness (activation) in addition to functioning in REM sleep. PPI deficits in patients with schizophrenia correlate with distractability [15]. This test, which measures inhibitory failure, does not directly provide information about cortical evoked potentials.

3—P50: When a sound (click) is presented one-half second after a similar sound, the second P50 evoked potential is reduced in amplitude. It is argued that the first stimulus initiates inhibition, which is tested by the second click and displayed by its P50 evoked potential. In schizophrenic patients, P50 suppression to the second click is diminished. That is, the evoked potential of the second click is greater in amplitude than in controls, indicating a lack of inhibition. If this can be extrapolated to the real world, it would be concordant with the behavioral manifestations of lack of suppression of irrelevant stimuli from the ambient surround.

Can a unified rationale for these three tests be suggested which will accord with the clinical observations of hyperawareness in the schizophrenia patient? PPI and P50 tests indicate a lack of inhibition of a test response by a preceding stimulus allowing for hyperawareness of the test stimulus in comparison with the normal individual. Can MMN be made to fit this template? A conceivable explanation relates to lack of habituation. Ordinarily, a frequently repeated event, such as the standard tone of MMN (repeated every half-second), will evoke less and less response—called habituation—presumably induced by an inhibitory mechanism. If there is a failure of this inhibitory network, as must be assumed for PPI and P50, the persistent background noise is the context in which the deviant test tone must be assessed. The contrast between test and surround is reduced and response to the test tone follows suit. Think of the retina as an analogy where "off cells" increase the contrast produced by the stimulated "on cells".

All this is of interest but does not refer to late event related cortical potentials, which correlate with self-consciousness [10].

Indeed MMN and PPI are specifically noted to be pre-attentive. The transition period (10-50 mS) from subcortical to cortical processing—presumably a pre-attentive period—is referred to as the middle latency period (12). Response onset for MMN may be 50 ms following the "challenge" stimulus with peak occurring at 150-200 mS. The startle response, as measured by contraction of the orbicularis oculi occurs within the first 250 mS following stimulus. It hardly needs to be emphasized that this is not a cortical evoked potential although it may be associated with an earlier one. If the behavioral observations of a hyperattentive awareness in schizophrenia have an objective correlate it would be well to look for it in the late event related cortical phase rather than the earlier period explored by these studies.

Perhaps some conclusions relative to the hyperattentive state can be extracted from the masking studies. In a study of backward visual masking, it was found that schizophrenic patients require a longer interval between stimulus and mask than normal controls to identify the stimulus [18]. One interpretation could be that therefore the mask is more intrusive in the perceptual process in schizophrenia than in the normal. That is, the patient is hyperattentive to the mask. Schizophrenia patients showed abnormality of forward auditory masking requiring an increased amplitude for the test tone to come to consciousness. This need for a higher signal to noise ratio implies a greater intrusion into consciousness of the noise (mask) in accord with the behavioral observation of hyperawareness of the irrelevant. ". . . forward masking consists of shaping the acoustical input by mainly DCN" (dorsal cochlear nucleus) "in line with evolutionary demands for suppression of redundant information, especially of successive more or less insignificant elements" [19]. The reference to the dorsal cochlear nucleus is of interest for there are reports of abnormal brainstem auditory evoked potentials in hallucinating patients [20] with lower brainstem and midbrain implicated [21].

The relevance of all of this to schizophrenia is that if the postulate of hyperawareness in the schizophrenic has value—as suggested by the verbalization of irrelevant (to the nonpsychotic) environmental stimuli—this should be testable. The ability by the patient to verbally acknowledge these subliminal events implies an associated late event related cortical potential. Employing a group of schizophrenic patients and a group of normal controls, response to a subliminal stimulus of increasing duration or amplitude can be used to measure at what level the late cortical event related potential appears. The problem will be to find an unmedicated cohort—truly psychopharmacologically naïve patients—for the effect of psychotropic agents may be long lasting after therapy is discontinued. Stimuli should be visual and auditory and be structured (a visual word or scene or a spoken word or phrase) or unstructured (flash of light, burst of tone or other sound). They should not be limited to auditory which have been studied extensively in schizophrenia (MMN, PPI, P300) because auditory hallucination may be a marker for a specific abnormality of the auditory system rather than an indicator of a general defect, which can be explored by a second modality such as visual. Threshold can be sought with increasing duration of a stimulus of constant suprathreshold intensity or with increasing amplitude (brightness or loudness) of constant suprathreshold duration. According to the hypothesis, the schizophrenic patient should show appearance of cortical late event related potential at lower amplitude or shorter duration than the normal control, although the artificial simple stimulus structure does not truly equate with the myriad of stimuli that mercilessly impinge on us in the real world.

Chapter 5

Conclusion

Consciousness, although hard to define, is manifest by behavioral responses of a biological system to environmental stimuli. It exists in intransitive form as vigilance, even in the absence of behavioral response, as, for example, (extending the customary definition) when the organism is asleep. When a response is produced (the transitive form of consciousness), the stimulus may be preverbal, referred to (for convenience) as subliminal or it may be verbalizable. These two forms of transitive consciousness, termed consciousness and self-consciousness, are accompanied by awareness and by awareness of awareness respectively. Awareness is manifested by nonlingustic behavioral response for which the presence of the stimulus cannot be verbalized. This level of behavior occurs in all of us as when, for example, a hand is withdrawn from a hot object before the heat is "felt" or a dropped object is caught "reflexively". The racer starts running before "hearing" the starting gun.

Clinical observation suggests the schizophrenia patient is hyperaware. Irrelevant stimuli that would ordinarily be subliminal intrude into language. This intensification of awareness may represent increased activation of the ascending reticular system or suppression of a higher level behavioral (as contrasted with cellular) inhibitory system. In either case, stimuli that ordinarily are not recognized play an unwanted role in social behavior, interpreted by society as symptoms of psychosis.

The two levels of transitive consciousness are accompanied by temporally separated evoked potentials that offer objective verification of their existence. Consciousness is accompanied by an early event related potential and self-consciousness is correlated with an additional, and later appearing, late event related response. If schizophrenia is a manifestation of (or at least accompanied by) a hyperattentive state, the prediction would be that stimuli that were ordinarily subliminal would generate a late event related potential as an electrophysiologic reflection of awareness of awareness signaled linguistically. This electrographic finding would serve as a surrogate for what happens in the real world and might point the way to new forms of pharmacotherapy.

Chapter 6

Reprise

Schizophrenia, as defined by clinical criteria, includes manifestations of a hyperattentive state. Irrelevant stimuli from the ambient environment intrude into language and other behaviors. These so called subliminal stimuli become liminal; they cross a threshold that allows them to be verbalized. It is that threshold that distinguishes self-consciousness—consciousness of itself—from consciousness. If a stimulus evokes a response, (and to be a stimulus it must evoke a response from a biological system, for stimulus is defined by response) it must have reached consciousness (or awareness) at some level, whether or not the organism can acknowledge its presence linguistically. Consciousness therefore is defined by how it is measured; consciousness without self-consciousness (awareness without awareness of itself) is still consciousness even if it be verbally denied, and is measured only by non-linguistic behavior. Verbal denial accompanied by nonverbal response constitutes the criterion for a "subliminal" stimulus. These two levels of consciousness, verbal and nonverbal, liminal and subliminal, self-conscious and conscious, are associated with two periods of electrographic potentials. The early and middle periods of evoked responses are not associated with self-consciousness; they cannot be verbalized; they are subliminal. The late event related potential accompanies self-consciousness.

If the schizophrenic patient is hyperaware, as clinical observation suggests, that is, if so called subliminal stimuli become liminal and can be verbalized, they should be accompanied by late event related potentials not evident in a group of normal controls. Using pharmacologically naive patients and matched controls the cortical evoked responses to a graded series of stimuli can be assessed. Separate studies of visual and auditory signals of fixed suprathreshold duration and of increasing amplitude (from well below threshold to well above threshold) should be employed, as should suprathreshold amplitude stimuli of increasing duration. In the hyperattentive schizophrenia patients, the postulate is that the threshold for verbalized recognition and for late event-related potential will be significantly lower than in controls.

References

(1) Miller, G. and Holden, C.: Proposed Revisions to Psychiatry's Canon Revealed. Science 2010, volume 327, pages 770-771.

(2) Lettvin, J.Y., Maturana, H.R., McCulloch, W.S., and Pitts, W.H.: What the Frog's Eye Tells the Frog's Brain. Proc. IRE 1959, volume 47, pages 1940-1951.

(3) Kaschube, M., Schnabel, M., Löwel, S., Coppola, D.M. et al: Universality in the Evolution of Orientation Columns in the Visual Cortex. Science, 2010, volume 330, pages 1113-1116.

(4) Locke, S.: Consciousness, Self-Consciousness and the Science of Being Human. 2008, Praeger, Westport, Connecticut.

(5) Baldesserini, R.J., and Lapinski, J.F.: Schizophrenia in Principles of Internal Medicine, 1977, Eighth Edition, McGraw Hill, New York.

(6) Turetsky, B.I. et al: Neurophysiological Endophenotypes of Schizophrenia: The Viability of Selected Candidate Measures. Schizophrenia Bulletin 2007, volume 33, pages 69-94.

(7) Penfield, W. and Jasper, H.: Epilepsy and the Functional Anatomy of the Human Brain, 1954, Little Brown and Company, Boston, Massachusetts.

(8) Locke, S, Caplan, D. and Kellar, L.: A Study in Neurolinguistics, 1973, C.C.Thomas, Springfield, Illinois.

(9)   Dehaene, S. et al: Consciousness and Subliminal Conflicts in Normal Subjects and Patients with Schizophrenia: The Role of the Anterior Cingulate, PANS 2003, Volume 100, pages 13722-13727.

(10) Libet, B.: Responses of Human Somatosensory Cortex to Stimuli Below Threshold for Conscious Sensation, Science 1967, Volume 158, pages 1597-1600.

(11) Del Cul, A., Bailet, S., and Dehaene, S.: Brain Dynamics Underlying the Nonlinear Threshold for Access to Consciousness, PloS Biology 2007, Volume 5, pages 2408-2423.

(12) Leavitt, V.M., Ritter, M.S., Foxe, S.M.: Auditory Processing in schizophrenia during middle Latency Period (10-50 mS). High Density Electrical Mapping and Source Analysis Reveals Subcortical Antecedents to Early Cortical Deficits. J. Psychiat. Neurosci. 2007, Volume 32, (5) 339-353.

(13) Keshevan, M.S. et al: Schizophrenia: Just the Facts: What We Know in 2008. Neurobiology Schizophrenia Research 2008, Volume 106, 89-107.

(14) Braff, D.L., and Light, G.A.: Preattentional and Attentional Cognitive Defects as Targets for Treating Schizophrenia, Psychopharmacology 2004, Volume 174, pages 75-85.

(15) Karper, L.P. et al: Preliminary Evidence of an Association Between Sensorimotor Gating and Distractability in Psychosis. Journal Neuro. Psychiat. Clin. Neurosci. 1996, Volume 8, pages 60-66.

(16) Meincke, U. et al: Prepulse Inhibition of the Acoustically Evoked Startle Reflex in Patients with an Acute Schizophrenic Psychosis—A Longitudinal study. E.U.A. Arch Psychiatry Clin. Neurosci. 2004, Volume 254, pages 415-421.

(17) Swerdlow, N. and Geyer, M.A.: Prepluse Inhibition of Acoustic Startle in Rats After Lesions of the Pedunculopontine Tegmental Nucleus. Behav. Neurosci. 1993, Vol. 107, pages 104-117.

(18) Del Cul, Dehaene, S. and Leboyer, M.: Preserved Subliminal Processing and Impaired Conscious Access in Schizophrenia. Arch Gen. Psychiat. 2006, Volume 63, pages 1313-1323.

(19) Källstrand, J. et al: Auditory Masking Experiments in Schizophrenia, Psychiatry Research 2002, Volume 113, 115-125.

(20) Lindstrom, L. et al: Abnormal Auditory Brain-Stem Responses in Hallucinating Schizophrenic Patients. Brit J. Psychiat. 1987, Volume 151, page 9-14.

(21) Igata, M. et al: Missing Peaks in Auditory Brainstem Responses and Negative Symptoms in Schizophrenia. Jpn J. Psychiatry Neurol. 1994, Volume 48, pages 571-578.